Five Gates of Entry: Selected Poems

Also by Don Langford

*In the Light of the Full Moon: Dispersions, Glimpses, and Reflections*

*Songs from Deep Time*

*Dwelling in the Twilight Realm*

*Water Rock Time*

*Fragrant Blossoms, Fading Light*

# Five Gates of Entry:
# Selected Poems

**Don Langford**

Published by D S Langford Publishing
Columbus, OH 43229
https://dslangfordpublishing.com

Printed in the United States

Cover art design by Don Langford

Names: Langford, Don, author
Title: *Five Gates of Entry - Selected Poems* / Don Langford

ISBN 979-8-9910480-1-9 (hardback)
ISBN 979-8-9910480-2-6 (paperback)
ISBN 979-8-9910480-3-3 (ebook)

Library of Congress Control Number: 2024919563

First Printing, October 2024

*For David,*
Son, Friend, and Inspiration

# Contents

from

### *Dwelling in the Twilight Realm*

from

### *Water Rock Time*

-----------------------------------------------------------------------

from
*Fragrant Blossoms, Fading Light*

Selected Somonkas

from

*In the Light of the Full Moon:*
*Dispersions, Glimpses, and Reflections*

## The Landlord Next Door

Patching a crack in the walkway,
filling a small hole in his house
with cement, returning a cup of soil
to a hole left in the ground by squirrels,
the old man, my landlord, works
                              patiently.

The world's calamities can wait;
he harvests the tomatoes that he planted
from seed, waters the impatiens that grow
in fullest bright color by his porch,
turns the earth and worms in his garbage can of rich
                              dark soil.

He will disappear some days with his fishing pole
and box of floaters and sinkers, and a lunchbox;
he will disappear with the squirrel cage that he uses
to relocate squirrels to other wooded places,
perpetually moving each generation that moves into our
                              neighborhood.

He will disappear
and the world that never knew he was here
will be smaller because of his disappearance.
He will leave no big mark that he was here;
he tends to his lawn, removing the weeds
each spring and fall,
        the humblest of souls
        taking the littlest portions from this world
        and returning them back to the earth,
        working deliberately and slowly,
        keeping his little part of the world from falling apart.

## In Amber

Sealed in amber, fellow traveler, you
will outlast my dust when it is all said
              and done;

Your curved spine, still pliant
one would guess, after a hundred million years,
resting inside a golden chamber
that will preserve you
until insects again reign on this worn earth.

The fossilized remnants of my species
will contain the heaviest metals we could mine
and synthesize, outlasting our strongest bones,
buried deep in canisters so no eye would look upon
their painful promise that change
and rapid mutation
are encapsulated inside
our death chambers.

The seed that flies over the seas, resting
its paper wings on the waves
before flying away again
on the warm currents of air,
contains in it all that is needed for earth and water
to transform it into full-grown tree or vine
or vibrant flower clinging to a rocky windswept crag.

Contained in the cocoon, the interim
of life that passes from land to air.
Pods of life, carrying all the travelers to other places,
journeys without destination, unfolding change,
grabbing hold of life in a new home of sun and wind.

There will be remote galaxies
visited by my species in the years to come,
but could those travelers ever return with anything as beautiful
as your webbed wing magnified in amber, a reminder
of what exists no more,
the wisp of life's golden glow on this earth.

## Autumn

The earth is turning its sunburnt cheek
toward our eyes, showing its deepest red foliage
at the tops of maples, the wide-awake yellows
filling our field of vision in the birch groves,
pulling the sap inward for another season.

Has it been a year already, we ask each other
on our ride through the mountains
to catch the fading sun on these shortened days.
When we were young we lay for hours in the dry
mouldering piles of crackling leaves, our rakes
leaned against the trunks of trees, we laughing and
telling stories that we would never again remember
or tell.  What we remember is the smell of earth
in those leaves and how we felt so much alive
in those bright piles of season's end.

And today, too, we stop and wade ankle-deep
in the still-bright leaves gathered on the forest floor,
seeing our breath in the morning sunlight air,
removing a leafy fragment from our hair, brushing off
twigs that hold to us, and we talk again about things of
little consequence in the presence of a world too big
for us to understand, cradled in its last warm leaves of the season.

## Sand Painting

Gather a handful of ochre stone
      from the vein on the mountain
      across the valley,
grind it with mortar and pestle
to smooth chalk the color of the back of your hand
      in fading sunlight,
and place the powder in a jar until all the colors
      for the sand painting are thus gathered.

Find the white of rib-bone in the desert mesa
where thousands of years have been pressed into
      a sliver that runs like the path of meteorites
      angled down into the earth
          from the wedge of mountain;
      scrape the hard whiteness with your fingernails
      rubbing it into the thimbleful of white that will
          be in the northern skull.

All day for seven days
gather and grind the deposits of rock
from this desert valley and mountain home,
assembling them for the mandala
where heart and mind join in vision—
symbols of the ancestors,
colors and signs,
a cosmology of meaning manifested in dust.

Impermanence and tradition
shared in the sand painting, days of quiet attention,
each movement and gesture ceremonial,
rooted in wisdom of the past
like the grain of mineral blue
flecked in the mountainside, hidden beneath the overhang
      of ledges;

At the end of days, the work is done, the connection between
the earth's colors and the passing moment linked;
wipe the sand painting from its recognized patterns
     and symbols
     into undifferentiated unity again, gather the sand
in a cloth satchel, carry it back to the overhang,
and release it into the wind, or into the river, returning it
to mingle again with the elements.

## Yellow Potted Flower

Do not offer consolation
    to the flower
    that opens only in the morning
    and closes its petals through the day.

Do not remind the flower
    what it is missing
    at the sun's zenith
    or what the long summer day displays
    to those who witness it.

Marvel instead at the mystery
    of its modest display
    and be present
    when it welcomes you at dawn.

Its grass-like leaves and narrow stem
    emerge from bulb
    growing skyward
    following the course
    of its own adaptations.

It has restrained its urges
    to grow like the others
    and makes no demands
    for special soils or light.

## Looking Seaward

In the bright light
slight right of where we stand
looking to sea
over scalloped waves,
we see islands of dolphins
bobbing in curves of shiny gray,
arcing beyond our reach.

We marvel at their seaward gestures
from our sandy cove,
feet planted firmly.

Once that was our home, too,
aqueous, evanescent—

there was coral for our backbones
in the food-rich sea . . .

What sea monsters
drove us from sea to tree tops?

Legless sea elephants, manatees
sprouted legs in the estuaries

sea lettuce growing
            on trees

sirens calling the sea-dwellers landward

until their feet
were firmly planted,
            yearning for seaward buoyancy.

# What the Dolphins Taught Me

Remember to breathe.

## On Visiting a Friend in the
## Camarillo Mental Institution

Is this what you wanted when you said,
"I am going to discover myself," and
began peeling away layer after layer from above
your high cheekbones,
pulling away the bones until the mirror
reflected only light?

Is this what you wanted when you said
there would be no more suffering,
no more to look for; no more looker?
Would clear white light have ever been enough for you?
They tell me you cannot hear your own howls at night—that you
have created a new language of wind and thunder;
that you have an eerie moan like someone who
has lost his way home—like someone who has too closely
seen the horrors of being human;
like someone imprisoned forever.

The nurse has said that you are trapped
inside a bag of skin, and that
it is too bad that I can't take you over to the window
and push you through the bars and release you
from this torment.

But, for another hour you and I sit together
in the filtered light.
I console myself with the thought that maybe
the blank stare on your face is really
supreme patience;
that you have already vacated this empty shell; that
we are merely propping pillows against the husk of a free spirit,
and that you, my dear friend, have left us
to make our own discoveries.

## Whispering Cottonwoods
(In memory of my sister)

If I said the bare cottonwoods in the moonlit winter night
looked like long fingers pointing upward, seeking something,
      would you follow my thought in silence
        to her hospital bed two months ago
when her warm bony fingers rested weightless in my hand?


How could you know I'm not thinking of the cottonwoods,
      or the glazed snow under moonlight,
but instead absorbing myself in those last hours with her?

We conceal worlds within our silences,
      or behind the brief whispered utterances.


When she became too tired to speak, I washed her hands
      with a warm wash cloth, hands that I then knew
      would never grow wrinkled with old age.

We did not discuss death, hope, or regret
      during those precious days
      of lingering lucidity.
      We let those hours slip by.


So much of what's real remains silent
      so much of what could have been said
      will remain forever unspoken.

Continents of meaning never to be uncovered.
      We talked, instead, of the commonplace
      and forgettable details of the moment.

There were opportunities to try to unravel how it came
        to this, the slipping away of it all.
        We said "I love you" to each other,
        and maybe that is enough.

The nurses came for blood, for pulse, for a distraction.

A week after I returned home across the country
        she sighed her last breath alone,
        leaving a half smile for her mother and father.

I will sit beneath the cottonwoods in the coming summer,
        hear her fading laughter, and count her first birthday missed,
        without a word to anyone.

## Chuang Tzu and the Culture of Appropriate Suffering

Chuang Tzu cried and sobbed alone when his wife died;
he did not display his mourning in public,
and when he had paid his respects to his wife
and the life they had shared for many years,
he beat on his pots and pans,
drumming through the night,
carrying on loudly, annoying the neighbors
who thought how disrespectful of a man whose wife had just died.

He should go into silent retreat, they thought;
he should remain downcast and solemn for some time
to display the proper degree of suffering.

When asked how he could be so disrespectful and playful
with death still in the air, Chuang Tzu said that he had mourned
naturally at his wife's death, and for a time he was saddened,
but how much more disrespectful it would have been to her
for him to carry on selfishly in his own grief, he said.
For her, too, he would get on with his life,
for he would not be mourning if she was with him;
why should he mourn for his own loneliness
when they had so many pleasant years together.
What was to be gained from prolonging the sorrow and self pity?

How disrespectful it would have been
to do anything other than experience joy in this life
and show it by beating on his pots and pans,
drumming through the night.

## Vivid Dreams, Antarctica

I.
Dearest love,

Here Man Ray photographs Matisse
        for an audience—
and Brassai, the "eye of Paris,"
sets up his camera
for a nightlife scene at the base of Mt. Erebus—
misty clouds swirling
        around bowler hats
                suspended in space

        hovering above base camp
invitations posted:        The Surrealist Ball
                        This Saturday Night
                        on the Ross Sea ice shelf . . .

White rabbits the size of caribou
turn to confetti,
all photographs are impounded,
marked NOT FOR EXPORT

"No one will believe the vivid dreams
        these folks are having down here"
—the only radio message sneaked out—

Emanations from the polar caps
planetary forces—we must be all right, my love.
This is what we must believe.

II.
Dearest Love—

Great Paleolithic band of wanderers here
                              this week
just passing through, like us,
visiting and talking around the fire—
rumors of warm underground lakes further on
                    forests and brown bears
                    beyond the distant ridge

This is no experiment, I heard someone say,
frozen beard breaking in his lap.
Another, wrapped in blue gortex
cried salty tears, fogging up his helmet.
What tribe is this?
Where is home?  Wilderness?
There must be a return,
          we all sobbed—
          a ceremony of weeping,
                    cleansing and purifying us
                    for the real trial.

We'll be all right, said our letter carrier,
returning, again, my latest letter to you.

III.
Dearest love,

          Spectral hieroglyphics—
                    positively dazzling . . .

The sea of love
          is frozen again today;
There will NO BATHING signs posted
                    at the top of ice sheets
                    1500 feet high,

29

roads dynamited up to the heights
        where we perch like space-age penguins
facing the sun
sitting like Buddhas
in a row
at peace for this eternal moment.
One of the penguins turned to me and said,
"This is the real world."
We all hallucinate together here.
        Good band of friends.
        This, they say, is how cultures start.


IV.
Leariest Dove,

A reindeer leapt,
        and took a bite out of the moon

Mad for love, leaving the world out of joint
                  —off kilter—
There are scouts
in geosynchronous orbit
        watching our every move from above
            —a celestial panoptic eye
        scoping us out, checking us twice
        something something something
        whether we're naughty or nice . . .

There'll be no Santa in this winter dreamscape
        Kurtz he dead
        Curtsie and goo-night, Bill
        Goo-night Loo
        Goo-night              Goo-night.

## Seismic Vertical

*— the point upon the earth's surface*
*vertically over the center of effort*
*or focal point, whence the earthquake's impulse proceeds,*
*or the vertical line connecting these two points—*

Could we have known there were signs
in the motion of birds,
        the dog's ears,
         and the crickets' silence—
that beneath the calm surface of things
      our lives were trembling—
          breaking up—
             rolling out of control?

Directly over the blind and silent fury
we lived our lives
as if these gentle contours of hill and valley
were something constant—
like unchanging friend, always there
to measure our shifting temperament,
      youthful folly,
        mid-life anxieties . . .

  always there to give the illusion
  that our disbelief in the solid unity
  and wholeness of things
  was itself an illusion.

For as long as these mountains and ravines
through which we have walked
these many years
remain still
amid the seasonal changes,
there would be for us

31

an ordered world
restrained by some logic to prevent it
from whirling into unexplained chaos.


But today, the winter trees might well have
sprouted wings and flown south
    like late arboreal geese;
the streams and pools that cooled us in summer
might just as well have boiled away
    into blue mist, leaving
      only a faint taste on our lips
          of ever having been here.
We did not read the signs;
there were no dung beetles to raise their antennae
to the charge of buffalo;
no noticeable formation of ice cracks
    in the standing water
      that would alert us to impending
          violent earth shake.


We were talking about the drives we once made
    along the winding California coastline,
ferns and foxglove in dew-laden summer mornings,
    along the steep ravines that dropped to the sea.
That's how blood vessels burst
      in one's brain
they say,—or in one's heart—
    waiting quietly, then exploding
      in the moment of calm,
as when you and I were caught in that green reminiscence,
      the quiet nostalgia
         of comfort in our own time,
not really thinking that this would last forever,
  but not believing that it could so suddenly roll over
  into something unimaginable,
    and vanish while we watched.

## Singing in the Key of Z

We will celebrate these reverberations
        these deflections
                of light and surface
the ricocheting of what we mean—
    like glints
    and scraps that never
                congeal,
                coalesce.


    We will come to admire
the fractured places
            —the interstices—
                that look like pursed smiles
                        on the cobbled walkway,
or the line of a closed eye
pressing out the light;

kaleidoscopic color chips
rubbing their cubist
    edges
            running round,
                cylindered
    and
            boxed in.

We grow content with the glaze,
                        the chips of colored glass, and
the way they float
    without history
            or meaning . . . over the scenery,
    cascading down from the overpasses,
    punched into smithereens
    like windshields crystallized . . .

we are bedazzled
by the world turning to powder,

           by our own
private minds, thinking
more alike,
entertained
                      beyond our wildest expectations—
thrilled numb
singing in our fashionable ennui
          before sleep.

## Intelligence in This Unfurling Moment

Aspen grove, a single organism,
     a community appearing as separate trees,
     leaves quaking in the well-watered hillside
     growing where the valley's nutrients
     will last hundreds of years.

Underground mycelium communities
     spreading nodes of communication
     in mats of subterranean fungal forest
     adapted to the mild earthy conditions.

Tropical cutter ants following the scent
     for the task they perform;
     no one in charge as the work gets done—
     chopping, transporting, building their city of tunnels,
     working for the benefit of the community
     that they cannot see from their own local vantage point.

A global network of human brains
     advancing without conscious direction;
     a complex organization of connections
     working out what it is going to be in its corner of the galaxy.

Cells awaiting differentiation
     awaiting the code assignments for specialization
     of what they will become.

We glimpse with awe the self-organizing intelligence
     all around and within us; observing for a moment
     our illusory separateness—

     being pulled by self-governing momentum
     toward some understanding that awaits us,
     awareness already contained in this unfurling moment.

## Sirens and Muses

Along the shoals,
with irresistible calls
and promises of pleasure or safety,
the temptress lures
the offshore sailors
who struggle in the foamy waves.

The witless sailors, entranced and confused,
unmoored from their old yearnings of home
feel only the inviting landward pull
of the sirens.

No longer heeding the voices of reason
or the inner compass
that reads to them the consequences
of their actions,
they turn their ships to land
and the fates that await them
in the foamy lather of sea waves
dashing on the slicing rocks
that splinter the water-logged ships
and toss the crew to their seaward grave.

The muse does not call
so insistently from afar;
she waits quietly, but willingly,
from within for the mind to be calm and still.
Like the magma working its way
through open fissures to the surface,
the words and ideas rise
as if beckoned from another place.
There is no crashing and thrashing
in the presence of the muse;
a quiet focus is required or
the inchoate ideas dissolve in the ether.

Like the oracle at Delphi
she may coax out the language in riddles
rather than insights
so even the writer on the shore of ideas
becomes the observing participant
in the co-creation of meaning
while watching them take shape before one's
own open eyes.

# Resuming the Search

We searched the archives
>to see if we had been here before
>maybe some stone carvings would provide a clue
>or maybe a clay mask would fit my face perfectly.

Perhaps some petroglyphs would indicate a neighboring
>clan that we could recognize as an old neighbor
>or we might find a burial shroud
>with the imprint of your deep eye sockets
>>and high cheekbones.

We sought some recognizable shard or urn
>we used for storing freshly pressed oil
>when we inhabited the fertile desert.

Going further back we searched the rocky mountainside
>for fossils of our fish forebears
>and we looked in the tar pits
>to see if we may have been trapped and preserved by surprise.

We excavated the depths of volcanic ash
>for a hint of how we once lived in community

and we studied the fossilized leaves that would have been our food
>when we lived among the treetops.

We collected and filed the tracings
>of where we likely swam and roamed long ago
>in so many places we called home

and now we sift again among the collections we gathered,
>mapping out the most likely course that led us here,
>trying to retrace our steps
>to see if all those clues

might tell us where we're going.
Future in the Present

To test whether there is a future
  we visualized a time when we would travel
  to the blue zones
  and we saw health and warm sand
  in the wispy salt air;

  we imagined cool afternoon breezes
    accompanying the fragrant taste
    of papaya and bananas;

  soon we saw ourselves planning,
  bringing our present toward the future,
  remembering that this, too, would be impermanent—
  as we flowed in a current that we were not controlling.

And we reached the sandy coast and the sun—
  as warm and comforting as we could ever imagine—
  and in the knowing that these days too would end,
  we did not prolong or attempt to repeat those moments,
  but with gratitude we looked on,
    glimpsing equanimity in the moving present
    like the movement of breaking waves
    in the ocean's stillness.

**Meeting the Deep Past in Burro Creek**

I stand
as representative
of earth's self-reflecting consciousness
in the desert of the American Southwest

Full moon rising over morning canyon
reflecting the sun's light faintly
against the layered canyon walls
—a message of earth's aging contained at a fault line
        of tectonic subduction

I stare at one speckled granite rock before me
itself containing all that I need to know
but do not understand

Among the boulders in the upthrust
this one is rounded smooth
with two deep holes like eye sockets
burrowed, one might guess,
by the slow and constant dripping of water
for a duration far beyond human time

Before speaking, I run my fingers into
the deep circular tubes
worn smooth in hardest rock
by the dripping of soft silky water

"Dear modest old rock, resting here for a time,
        wearing down so slowly that
        all of humanity could walk by
        and say good morning—
        I have come here to learn patience and perseverance."

from

*Songs from Deep Time*

## Hands of My Ancestors

These hands—reptilian-creased with age—
        borrowed shape and bone from ancestors
        all the way back to tiny tree-dwellers—and beyond,
        who grasped and scratched
                on continents far away from here

                each living its own lifetime
                toiling in sun and rain
                unaware of the generations before
                        and after

                unaware of continents slowly drifting
                ice ages coming and going
                cataclysmic earth events
                while the hands grasped
                for food
                        for comfort
                                for a way forward

                one day at a time

                passing along the code
                        the genetic baton
                        one generation at a time
                        millennia after millennia

While these hands opened and closed
        cupping to carry water to share with others
        becoming tool makers
        learning to wave and weave stories
                around fire

scratching out new ways to clamber
over the earth
ever searching, clasping

And now these hands
—look at them—
resting still;
fingers interwoven in gratitude
for having come all this way.

## Appearing and Dissolving
(In memory of Barbara Hancock, 1928-2022)

Out of the ocean
      a wave appears

wind and warm currents
      and a thousand conditions
      shape its form and movement

no clear beginning and ending
      it moves to shore with other waves
      some smaller, some larger
      some clear blue and curving
      some frothy and foam-filled

the wave approaches the shoreline
      appearing individual and separate
      as if running to shore
      on its own

some dissolve slowly over long sandy beaches,
      others make a dramatic crash against shoreline rocks;
      most glide ankle deep in their transformation

after their one run to shore,
their one curling rise,
      all the waves, with their differences
      and similarities,
      are pulled back into the sea
      in a dissolving return
      to the churning water
      from which they came

## The Warriors and the Poets

There were then
       as there are now
       the warriors who fought other warriors

       warriors who fought among themselves
       sometimes for justice or territory
            at times for power, social status—
            spreading the values of culture
       for conquest and riches
       plundering for glory,
            even achieving immortality
            in name and deed,
       recruiting the citizenry to honor violence
       cloaked in respect and acceptance.


There were then, as now, the poets
       and chroniclers speaking, then inscribing into culture
       higher aims of the human heart,
            a way forward out of the ashes
            and horrors of war,
       writing of other possibilities,
       devoting lives to de-romanticizing violence,
       seeking ways out of suffering,
       knowing that in response to bellicose assaults
            silence is not acceptance
            in the deliberate choice
            to live a quiet peace.

       Artists may wear the warrior's mask
            or melt the hardened armor,
            finding new expressive ways
            to pierce the human heart.

## Youth and Elder on the Trail

Youth and elder on the trail

young one races forward,
        energetic, bounding,
        full of new ideas

older one slowing gait and gaze,
        looking back, pondering,
        feeling bones and hardened rock

young one clambering, like mountain goat
        striding upward, much to do,
        summit to reach

older one has been to summits,
        now takes time to see the view,
        feel the warm sun, cool breeze

young one long ago respected elders,
        listened to wisdom tales,
        now looking to new adventures

older one once had wisdom to share,
        connections to make
        in a slower-moving world

young one looking forward
older one looking back
        each seeing the distance between them growing

## A Last Acceptance

Living long enough
we learn that every embrace
is a letting go

Saying goodbye
we look a little longer
into the other's eye

What we pull in close
will vanish in wind
and water flow

Even the words
uttered more slowly
conceal finality

There was just enough time
to catch the lightning strike
on the edge of our vision

Or feel the glow of sunlight
warming some elusive core,
a thought of who we are

We learned so little
from this borrowed chance,
just enough to live with wonder

And when the sun dropped
beneath the golden scrim
we rode the receding wave

## Far from Home

Poolside at Vichy Springs
two women from Belarus sat, food spread
across the table, wasps filling the air
and at the edge of the table
a little cake, a Proustian madeleine
set aside for the yellow jackets
to feast on in their own conversation.

From one angle the women were content,
undisturbed in their conversation,
occasional slow fanning of hands
to remind their flying visitors
that they could co-exist in peace,
enough sweets for all.

Sitting plump in their long dark dresses
they shared their custom of food
bringing sweet common comfort
to the quiet sun-filled resort
aloof from fashion or sunbathing
in their dignified picnic alone.

From another angle, far from home,
awaiting news, they shared what they knew
from family letters, memories of other times,
all the familiar places now unrecognizable,
holding on in this brief warm interlude.

In this snapshot across the blue water,
they sit at the intersection of uncertainty
and hope, cushioned by tradition
and quiet resilience, a determination
in their soft voices to live as if
the others will someday join them.

## Asymptote of Understanding

Spun out into this temporary locus
by the dust of stars
for only a brief blink of time
we try to gain a foothold,
       a perspective, a touchstone
       from which to gaze outward and inward.

Our eyes and hands extend far into space
and deep into the tiniest recesses
of our mental and physical selves.

Our questions move us deeper into the mysteries
of our existence, tempting us
to believe that each revelation
brings us closer to an understanding.

We sit on the shoreline
watching the waves come in, then recede;
all the laws of motion playing before us
in the constant action of foam and sand.

But this illusory appearance of constancy
is only impermanence in slow motion.

In the evanescence of certainty
we fall back gently, head to the sand,
eyes to the clouds
      of unknowing
         rolling over us,

sinking into the trust that this sandy earth will hold us,
and in this brief buoyancy
we surrender, letting go of effort,
confident that the stability of this shoreline

will hold us long enough
for the waves of enough-ness
to sweep over us like warm currents.

All the practice has brought us to this shore—
discipline and striving, purposeful effort,
the preparation and conditions for what follows:
sometimes a flash of insight,
sometimes another day of effortless dedication
through persistence and perseverance.

## Constant Striving

Each of us tethered to the colony
dreaming to float away
beyond the gravitational pull
      of our time
      and culture

to see what we glimpse in our dreams
when we climb into space
on filaments
that connect us
to deep time
before form and structure

a human voice or recognizable sound
breaks the fragile reverie
and we return again like a punctured balloon
from the place where we floated
in our mind

between the outward pull
and acceptance of our earthbound home
we hover for a moment in our dual state
of desire and resignation,
before spinning again in our descent toward earth
where we find ourselves after every dream

and we bounce back, recurrent
in our efforts, like moths
trying to reach the moon,
telling ourselves it is in our nature,
or believing that one day
it will be effortless
to arrive at a place where we have never been

from

*Dwelling in the Twilight Realm*

# Neighborhood Dream Cafe

We were counseled to remain silent about the loss
of our memories or any confusions that lingered
about the atrocities we had witnessed.

This we learned from anonymous notes
strewn about the cafe we visit on our nightly rounds,
and lipstick reminders adorning the mirrors in our hotel room.

Some of the messages we may have posted ourselves;
others, like those pinned to walls
or carved into the wooden tables
and bar tops, were intended to
sow doubt and mistrust among the patrons.

Cryptic messages were folded
into our serviettes, strychnine droplets in the coffee,
even the waiters averted their eyes
when we used their threatening notes as currency
to pay our bills.

We know they laughed like hyenas in the cafe kitchen
after we exited with leftovers dripping in our pockets.
We'll see who laughs when they discover what happened
to the quarters in the jukebox or the peppermints on the counter.

We have grown distracted by pettiness
while there are snipers in the streets and in the courts
picking us off one by one like sleepwalkers in an arcade.

In our consolation we return again each evening
to the same neighborhood cafe
never knowing what to expect,
never knowing if we will remember
what we did the night before.

## Another Day of the Dead

Festive afternoons of draped crepe paper
gave way to nightmarish evenings
where sleepwalkers in the cafe of lost dreams
pulled on the brims of their sombreros
beneath the white-boned skulls
decorating the darkened bar
on the Day of the Dead.

How is it not possible to know
that one is being haunted
by the glares from the coal-black eye sockets
shifting in the flickering light,
reminding the tequila drinkers
that their mothers and fathers
are patiently waiting in their graves
for something good to come
of the sons and daughters who abandoned them
in their late-life time of need?

The worm at the bottom, the hooked bait,
works its way into the skulls leaning against
the booth backs and brass bar rails,
eating from the inside the catch of the day.
The boisterous jesting, the happy backslapping,
and the early evening furtive eye gazing
turn to quiet somber catatonia
hours after the haunting inner voices
rise out from under the volcano,
and large insects crawl along the inner eyelids
where no one else sees them.

Soon they are walking along the bar top,
and across the mirror and walls,
large crusty-shelled and noisy, their staccato feet tapping

faster and louder, and the faces of the people at the bar look on accusingly
and yet oblivious to the clattering noise of the armadillo bugs
dodging behind the liquor bottles into the damp and darkened corners.

Elbows on the bar top, hands pressing tightly against the ears,
one and two, and then three grown men try to keep out the cries
of loved ones abandoned, helpless figures lying on the roadside,
reaching out their hands in a final pleading gesture.
Then the soft sobbing begins and the bartender looks at his watch;
still two hours before closing time and sending the day's catch
into the night where they will find a way to wipe away
guilt and loneliness until the gnawing brings them back again
for more. They will not remember the brief glimpses they had
of something rotting deep inside. The vagueness will be transformed
by the next afternoon into a need for camaraderie.

The faint smell of bleach, the mopped floors, the glossy bar top
welcome the return of the dwellers of forgotten nightmares,
and no one remembers the armadillo cockroaches crawling over their hands
and into their shirt sleeves. There's news and gossip to bring the patrons
together yet again, sipping the first round that, this time, may take them
closer to euphoria or the land of a new rising sun.

One of the men rubs a wet finger round and round
in little circles on the bar top, pressing it like a coiling spring
almost hypnotically, as if he is pushing something through,
then he slowly swirls the last mouthful at the bottom of his glass
and asks the bartender for another.

## The Sleepwalker

Guided by the voice
she shuffled through the darkened house,
robe draped over bony frame,
opening the window blinds—and waiting.

Who is coming this time?
Who will not arrive this time
        before she returns
        to forgetful sleep?

Beguiled by the calm night voice, her trusted huckster,
        she is no Cassandra.
We take her back to bed
not awaiting news from the future—no glimpses or premonitions;
        only the hope that she will sleep.

Only we will remember, at daybreak,
that she stood, convinced,
        at the window
        peering into darkness
        with an urgency . . .
                that someone was coming to see her
                and she must be there to greet them.

For her, in daylight, this never happened.
At the breakfast table she has no recollection.
Maybe it is only for us to witness
until someday, when we hear our own night voices
        calling to us of some urgent need,
        we may believe that our delusions are insights
                or that the events never happened at all.

## Ways to Say Goodbye

Drop all the petals at once
windblown end of season
        winter chill setting in
        the once vibrant colors
        no longer holding on
        letting go in a moment

A carefully written note
        held in place on the table
        with a token thank-you gift
        hinting of a later return
        —a jar of jam or sprig of mint—
        in early morning while everyone sleeps

Place a half-filled satchel by the door
        like a guest waiting for check-out time
        let the days ripen with conversation,
        slowly adding to the bulging pack,
        warm embraces before departure

Find a quiet place to lay down the bones
        like Jeffers' deer
        in sunny outcropping
        overlooking the sea,
        waves chanting in the background

## Over the Edge

At the edge of sleep on your own,
      leaning out over the abyss
      night after night,
      cremnophobia has invaded
      even the spaces
      where once you closed your
      eyes to the fears
            and the treatments
            that took you to the edges
                  of rooftops.

You sat blindfolded
on bridges over rivers,
      feeling the metal girders,
      hearing the flowing water below
      pulling you to your knees
            whimpering, babylike
            crying for solace.

In the canyon hikes
the guides walked on,
      leaving you clinging
      to a spindly tree trunk
      like an imploring lover
            panting on the overhang,
            "Do not leave me here alone."

And now you sit at the top of the carpeted stairs
      wide-eyed octogenarian
      after a lifetime of accomplishments
      calling out to an empty world,
      "Is there anyone down there
      who can help me?
      I'm about to fall again."

**Protecting the Little Turtles**

In the last dream
before dreaming ceased
   in endless sleeplessness

there was a line of tiny turtles
   crossing the road
and we joined the people
who were lifting or escorting them
to safety in the sandy coastal dunes
where they would lay their eggs

Cars raced by, honking horns
   and crushing dozens of turtles
   heedless of the efforts to save the slow-paced creatures

In the dream some of the people carried turtles to their safety,
   then derailed cars from the roadway,
   watching them careen into fiery piles
   or explode over cliff sides into the waiting sea

With sneering smiles some abandoned the turtles altogether
   to focus their efforts on dismantling the traffic
   that raced fiercely through the turtle crossing.

Some of the turtle protectors ripped out the roadway signs
   warning traffic of sharp turns ahead
   and even posted new signs
   that directed traffic over the embankment
   into the foamy sea

Waking from this last dream to the news of new human atrocities
   and the cruelties one inflicts on the unknown others,
   each with his or her own family to protect and love,
     each with a simple desire for safety

## Opening the Heart in Red Rock Canyon

You were reaching deep into the earth that day, pushing
up red hot fiery rock of living memory, describing your smothering
journey into blackness

> We moved slowly through the canyon
> that had thrown up red rock in early upheaval,
> reshaping itself, transforming the landscape
> into a jewel of light and life

You had moved beyond the reach of caring hearts
into the realm of the one-way dive
drinking the pitch black midnight
that boiled your brain and dried your desires for meaning

> We pulled into a turnout where you stood
> above the valley, smiling for a photo
> with cliffs behind you in the distance

You had pulled yourself down into the darkness
of the soul where loneliness feeds only on the company
of a self that has grown tired of moving on—
a world unhinged from any meaning,
nothing left but the letting go

> We looked at the landscape that had constantly renewed itself,
> juniper and barrel cactus healing the valley,
> sunlight warming the autumn earth

You had looked beyond the silver backing of the mirror
into the gulf beyond yourself, beyond any recognizable reflection,
and in that darkest death nudge where all desire and hope have vanished,
you washed your face and drank water, deep survival instinct awakening
out of the blackness beyond thought

We turned from one scenic overlook to another,
at times hearing only the sound of the breeze
blowing through dense desert brush that had learned
to survive on the morning dew, then
we headed home

You had turned back to life, responding to the shiver in your brain,
the wordless summons to begin the long journey home.

## The Still and Changing Sea

In this crossover world
of shared borrowings
tall Ponderosa pines drop their heavy cones
next to glossy-leafed Magnolias
shiny in the morning sun,
and palms grow in fanned clusters
near clumps of desert oat grasses
that spread toward the sandy dunes
and the smooth white sands of Florida's Gulf Coast.

This is a quiet world in December,
a few strolling visitors on the beach,
here by some unknown invitation,
some walking barefoot along the shoreline
carrying their shoes in curled fingers.

There is still mystery in the breaking waves,
unending in their hypnotic rhythm
the changing stillness
in its coming and going;
here, we are looking back at our first home
past the long ebb and flow of tides and time,
past all the differences and changes
that brought us here.

Near these calm shores
seekers and plunderers sought their fountains of youth,
pillagers racing and raging through
the source of life at their feet
It is here at the shore's edge
that the youth-giving mist of the sea
touches the land in its long caress;
it is here that the earth renews itself.

This wide and never-ending expanse of the sea
speaks its own ancient language
for the patient sea-farer to decipher
and the shore-wandering visitors to feel
in the quiet incessant music of its call

## What Do We Have to Say?

And for those of us
for whom calamity and catastrophe
have not touched our lives,
have we nothing to say
about the silent deaths in our family,
the usual kinds of malpractice in the hospital
or the neuropathies associated with alcohol
or the slow robbing of a mind by dementia?

These are the small individual earthquakes
that do not leave rubble in the streets.

These are the silent pains at the bedside
where there are no bombed out buildings
or bloodied bodies in the street.

We do not huddle with neighbors to share
        our grief and wailings.

We are alone with a father who is suffocating
        in a hospital room on Thanksgiving weekend
        when the part-time staff are laughing down the hall.

We are bent over a donated bed where a mother
        is sinking with her gray-skinned face
        into the last gurgling sleep,
        leaving us helpless at her bedside.

We are saying goodbye to a young sister
        who wears pink slippers on her painful feet
        saying to us don't worry, meaning she wants to go.

For those of us who grew up with the American Dream
        coming across the border from Canada,

living like the *Leave It to Beaver* family on TV,
uneventful immigrants like our forebears
from Ireland and Romania
who struggled in their own silent ways,
what do we have to say
in the quiet privilege we have fallen into?

We have no photographs or newspaper clippings
about devastation felt by thousands;
for that we marvel at our good fortune.

We are saddened by the catastrophes of nature
and the inhumanity of war
and the devastation that leaves millions
marked forever if they survive.

We watch quietly while we write our poems,
our imaginary escapes from something hidden,
little abstract wonderings, the aimless wanderings
of searching minds in the ephemeral clouds,
escaping from the end of the line,
driving in circles in a kind of orphaned freedom.

We have nothing to say except to create new echoes
that resound off the walls of our own experiences,
a tiny packet of papers for no one else to read;
just a few short volumes to say we, too, were here.

## Mother, Father, Sister

They have gone
this time forever
out of reach
          and beyond any calls

and still this sense of waiting

to share some news
little milestones
a closeness expressed
in morsels
so imaginatively small

we never thought about endings
when we had all the time
          in the world

sometimes wondering
what conversations we would have had
if we had a chance today
          knowing what we now know
          about death's insistent turn

and now untethered
in a kind of orphaned freedom
these unanswered calls
on days of remembrance
          are woven into the day
          like the cold November wind
          announcing another winter

## M Is for Love

Somewhere above this sublunary miasma
blue bejeweled Betelgeuse,
like wedding ring in the night sky,
        spins

conch shells spin too,
as does the old curled white pine
used for carving canes

and the sperm of whales and hominins
boring their way with pigtails swimming

cutting their way like rivers to the sea
leaving their curved and carved imprints
in the sandy waterswept inlets

rarely in a straight line
does water flow,
its course wandering
with the easy curves

this is the watercourse way
the way of galaxies
and the tendrils of bean and fern,
climbing and swirling toward
the open spaces.

And so with the old man bent forward,
lost in thought, looking for shells
or wandering in curving swirls on the sandy shore,
the first reflections of stars
through the watery pools in his eyes,
curved fingers gripping a cane,
fading memories swirling

in fragments and filaments
spinning loose into galaxies of thought,
heading toward the easy places,
gazing out to sea or inward
toward some sanctuary of retreat.

And in the gloaming
on the same sandy shore
he sees first an apparition before him
then the half familiar form
and the growing comfort he calls love,
he knows she is here to save him again
she is walking toward him
bringing a handful of shells
her smile and a warm curving hand
fingers now interlaced in his
guiding him along the easy shore
back to the home he had been looking for.

## Awakening from Long Sleep

During the long sleep
    we dreamed

We dreamed at first
    of manicured orchards in bloom
    and cloudless skies placed there
    for our own pleasure

For our own pleasures and amusements
    we dreamed

We dreamed of ease and comfort
    we dreamed of freedom for all
    when we dreamed beyond ourselves

When we sought the pleasures for ourselves
it blinded us from the suffering of our neighbors
    here and everywhere

And from our dreams we began to hear the refrain
    that it was time to awaken
    that it was long past time to awaken
    there was work to be done

For so long we dreamed on, harboring
    the old habits of comfort
    before the songs of resistance arrived

And out of our dreaming at long last
    the smallest seed was sown,
    the long-germinating humming and groaning
    and we began seeking a way forward

In the sweet rhythms we heard the calls
             of freedom songs
             calling us forward,
             time to rise up they sang
             in their soft insistence

Toward the sweet rhythms we climbed
             out of our dreamy sleep and slumber
             taking the first earnest steps forward

We had wandered long toward the precipice
             where the waking twilight realm
             meets the advancing night of dreams

And we knew, at last, that it was time
             to waken from the dreams
             that had guided us toward
             the blinding depths of unreason

Dante's infernal rings would have shaken us
             ever more quickly into the wakened state,
             but we had no such fears and flames
             in our dreamlike slumber

We took, instead, the long march
             not even knowing
             that we were on a path
                     or on a treadmill

We were guided by the choices we made,
             each turn with its own consequence,
             and not until we examined finally
             the conditions that brought us here
             did we admit that a crisis had arrived

The need to awaken was the natural urging
    that brought us forward willingly
    out of the twilight realm

And from this vantage point we peer into new spaces,
    another place for open-eyed poems
    where music of the heart
    waits for a further unfolding

from

*Water Rock Time*

## Desert Sky

Today, gentle rain
      tapping
      like children's fingers on the roof.

At sunset, the underside
      of folded clouds
      golden, rolling east
            over mountains
            and valley.

## Hot Mineral Bath

Cool morning
      in California desert
      sitting in hot mineral bath
      cradled in its warm liquid embrace

These steaming pools have deep thermal ties
      to ancient seas and molten ores

Water, flesh, and bone
      sharing common origins,
      flowing together for a time

## After the Rain

After the rain
children ride bicycles
through ruts and mud puddles
laughing and splashing,
barking at the dogs
to get them going

In the afternoon,
mud-caked boots
piled in a heap,
dirty bikes waiting
for another ride

## Returning to the Source

Standing at the headwaters of the Metolius,
water bubbling up,
leaking out of the ground
more of a trickle than a flow

Humble origins,
late bloomer from the north
like snow-ball rolling

gradual and persistent
growing on its downhill ride,
       someday arriving
           at the sea

# A Little Frozen Pond

We were children once,
and in the faintness of memory
there was a shallow pond
far back behind the house

We played in the bush
and in tall fragrant grasses
with our little dog

And there were wild pear trees
around the old concrete foundation
of a burned-out house
that we never tired of visiting;
a crumbling fireplace and chimney
reminded us that someone once lived there

When the small pond froze over
in the winter we put on our ice skates
and our caps and mittens
and stepped from the frozen golden grasses
on to the thick and crackling slab of ice
to play all afternoon
until our hands were numb
and the cuffs of our pants
were ice-caked in stiff frozen folds

Tell me, do children today
still toboggan down those old frozen roadways
or run aimlessly far from home
with their dogs through long carefree afternoons,
and in the summer
do they wait with dimes and quarters
clenched tightly in their hands
for the ice cream truck to arrive,

or hear the beverage truck bringing wooden crates
of mixed flavored pop, bottles jangling
all the way down the street,
straight to the house?

What are the safe and comforting memories
today's children will someday recall
of their own long-ago summers and winters?

# The Wateryness of Meaning

The watery-ness of words,
>fluid rivers of meaning,
>pooling concepts
>coursing recklessly toward obstruction,
>damming the range of flow

We try again, reiterating in iterative approximations,
>defending our claim:
>all utterances are not the sensations
>they attempt to translate;
>they do not equate or equivocate

Lost in the eddies that swirl
>around ideas and emotions;
>lost in the riptides that pull us
>>away from what is most important,
>>the fundamentals of our
>>>being here

The little rivulets we tried to follow
>long before any wordiness of vision
>>intervened, even interrupted,
>>occasionally contravened,
>>and even contested

Now the language interferes
>with where we want to go
>in this inquiry into the meaningful,
>>before the fragmentarians among us
>>tried to pull us apart

A disquisition of this sort, *in situ*, should dive deeply
       into the aqueous world of words, splitting molecules, if necessary,
       so hydrogen is liberated from its filial bond,
       hurtling closer toward pure meaning

We incubate a surrogate brood of words and images
       that have severed (cleaved if you like) the umbilical
       toward a more restrictive language that would have
           oxygen become the dominant bond-mate as water tumbles
           like bubbling plosives over riverbed stones to the sea

What we wanted, after all, was to have some wordless affirmation
       of our discourses, some semblance of watery resolution
           of our most consequential certainties
           in this ever-flow of wordiness

## Ontogeny of the Tendril

Beautiful green leaves
of palm and ficus

tall and broad
beyond the measure
    of climbing

pulling water upward
    into gravity's outer canopy

deep-rooted fibrous filaments
    collecting each its smallest portion
    gaining complexity with size

    like the ant colony
    building intricate tunnels
    beyond a single ant's ability

and we too send tendrils outward
    to moon and mars

    the capillaries
    of our human colony
    pushing star-ward
    beyond the bounds
    of our knowing

## Longing at Water's Edge

Why we return to the sea,
the mossy brook,
the lapping wavelets
at the lake's sandy shoreline

endless change
over the monotone surface
the glassy plain
that breeds the wild storms

the sameness pulls us in,
mesmerizing sound loops
cascade over river stones,
or ocean waves on sandy berms,
in slow watery heartbeat rhythms

old stuff, unremembered—
womb music, oneness undivided
longing without return—
we were jettisoned forever out of the waves

we wait on the shoreline
or swim in comforting shallows,
refreshed in this quiet detachment
disguised as home

## To Flatiron on Superstition Mountain

Trudging slowly up Siphon Draw
climbing over boulders, grabbing branches
firmly rooted in rock
      finding a toe-hold
      in the tumble packed tightly
            in the shaded canyon walls

Pulling, pushing, straining upward
      in aching exhaustion
      toward the goal of Flatiron
      standing high above
      against the blue sky

Resting, back against stone
      breathing hard
      high above valley
      and far-distant mountain ridges,
      for a moment before moving again upward

No need to reach the summit;
this could be enough,
but something pulls upward
      into the unknown

The rock hardens at mid-elevation
then higher up it crumbles
climbing upward through earth time here,
      layers of hot compressed core material
      steps of sharp squared blocks
      burning muscles
      hours of upward climbing

Other hikers point the way
        offer encouragement and water
        before the final hard push to the top

From atop Flatiron
        a distant view, enchanted exhaustion
                its own reward

Joyful satisfaction
        intense, momentary
        inscribed and etched deeply enough
                to go with me all the way
                        back down.

## Mountain Sand Granules

The granulated white sand
    on the beach
    we were told
        is granite

Wind and water, persistent,
    eroding solid mountain rock face
    to this fine white sand

On house-sized boulders
    young pine trees grow,
    soft and pliant roots
        burrowing deeply,
        cracking stone

On this wind-blown beach
    we are sprinkling old mountains
    from one hand to another

Tomorrow we climb up the gorge
    to mountain summit;
    granite boulders on the way
    to their destiny:
    beach sand piled high,
        sand dunes for sea oats

## Our Precipitous Rock Ledge

Resting in morning sun,
lizard-like in our stillness
most basic of animal postures
seated, elemental,
> on a rock
> overlooking
> deep green valley
> where trees stand quietly
> beneath an unforgiving sun

A lesson in patience, it may seem,
> from ridge to ridge
> out to some far distant horizon
> that invites our vision
> to look more closely

Some of the trees have been speaking out;
> this language we understand:
> blighted and dried out forests,
> bark-beetle dead for miles.

Others dry out, parched
> beyond endurance,
> a slow quiet dying
> far from our perch
> on the rock ledge,
> where we watch
> from this precipitous home

The pines are telegraphing to one another
> from root to root their signals
> of stress and disease

Others may yet go up in flames,
        sending toxic plumes
        as their final dying message

And we sit upon our silent rocky ledge,
        not yet ready to hear
        the urgent songs
        sounding all around us;
        not yet seeing the fibrous tree root filaments
        connected to the webbed branches
        of our own lungs

## Ondine and the Rock Outlasting

Ondine, aglow at nightfall,
dressed in deep subterranean blue,
eyes of ice painted with coal dust
and golden vapor, resting her heels,
nymph-like out of water, leaning
against the city rock at Town Creek
before the street widens

Even the wide-eyed children grin
past the rock, hiding giddy youthful stares,
not yet circumspect nor sheltered
by the lonely hearts yet undiscovered
that await their fading innocence and dreams

Hand stains and polished sheen
of kisses and fingers gloss the rock
that marks the center of town,
a history of sideways glances,
stealthy leanings, before the porticoes
of city hall were fashioned
and burned to the ground;
rock outlasting the comet's passing
and newspaper accounts
of the wealthy and the restless;
the music and fashion,
styles like the trees and their leaves,
bursting in color, fading into softness;
the rock waits in silence,
song birds wait their turn

## Pulverized Brick Dust

The morning teases
with its silhouettes
and curving folds
of curtains
in the straining light

They are pointing
to some outward place
where we wanted peace
even as the growing tumult
presaged war

So many bricks
taken from the growing rubble
like the boys sent far away,
disappearing around some corner
while new buildings rise
in the empty footprints

Ideas pulverized into red
brick dust, rock into powder,
fashioned into merchandise
with no burial ground large enough
to cover the memories
that rise like ghosts
from the steaming ground

In the lacy curtain's fold
turning slowly at the open window
a stirring breeze
meets hypnotic stare,
softens a broken heart
that waits for one who does not return

## Time's Reminders

There are reminders
in the sea waves on the sandy shore,
the broken antler found along a meadow's path,
even in the children's high-pitched laughter

All around us, in the slow drip of morning dew,
the rusted truck sinking in a grassy field,
the persistent cough of a loved one,
the exquisite beauty of colorful roadside flowers

We know there are endings of all that we love,
seasons bright with reminders
that we too will fade out of bloom
and perhaps remain for a time in someone's memory
before joining those countless unseen grains
that the sea waves sweep over
in a span far beyond our knowing

## Waiting for the Tide to Turn

we fed our solitude
           until
the tides receded

we asked ourselves,
who would want
this wondrous gloom,
with its green and scummy sound
racing into the nightfall

forgetting even the reason
for coming to this place
we asked ourselves one more time,

can we escape
before anyone finds us
measuring our skulls,
preparing for the long journey
           inland

## Evening at the Symphony

Violins, in their own language,
conveyed an anguish
that left us weeping.

How it transported us
      we do not know,
      but somehow,
      we knew this:

In time, our capacity to care
grew out of the pain
we observed in others.

Empathy and compassion
      rooted deep in ancient
      small wandering bands,
      led us to this evening's
      emotional tumult.

The orchestral strings tapped
on some human cord
like a symphonic tuning fork
adjusted to deep human sympathy
and we very quietly wept
those warm salty tears
and held back a choked
and convulsive breath.

The music of loss vibrated
inside of us in a recognition
that followed us all the way home.

We have cared for loved ones,
knowing all along
what the outcome would be.

We bottled our pain and loss
beneath a silent and stoic shell
until this evening,
when the violins in darkness
opened the chambers
of our guarded hearts,

and we sat until the early morning hours
at that same kitchen table
where so many remembered conversations
had occurred, unburdening the truths
that allowed us to move forward,
knowing that we did all
that we could have done
with no regrets.

## Regeneration

Like the deer, we wandered
deeper into the woods to heal

Sitting and settling in
has been our way,
whether inside in comfort
or on a canyon trail
remote and far away
from the home and family
we once knew

Maybe seeing that the world around us
continues to move along
allows us to adapt again to its slow and peaceful rhythms.
The cypress and cedar do not bend to our sorrows;
the doe and her only fawn have their own concerns;
this helps in our own healing, a solace without words;
seeing that life around us exists only in the present.

In time, the breathing comes easier,
we begin to see more of the outward manifestations
on our hikes through mountains and deserts,
instead of the inward focus, the heavy feeling
that blinds us from where we are.

Even in its own suffering,
the green and growing world around us
heals us in its example of quiet persistence.

Today we noticed the new green shoots
emerging from the ground
after the rain three days ago.

Already, we are moving forward once again.

## Content with No Words

Sometimes content
        with no words

warm sun and soft breeze
        silence the thoughts

palm fronds set against blue sky
        in stillness high above
        offering companionship

past and future
        out of view
        beyond the distant horizon

lying here with a half-smile
sloughing off body and mind
        not even waiting
                for change

## Late Night Cup of Tea

This contentedness may be fleeting, momentary,
    like the lull before
    the necessary occupations
    of the coming day

    but I am content with that
    at end of day
    feeling the tired calm
        that comes from working
        and walking

In our little house on wheels
    late at night
    I do a slow Tai-chi routine
    all incorrect and imitative,
    but flowing gently
    in comfort, alone
    a kind of slow jig for a tired man
    in a solitary moment

a calm conjuring of the muse
    while stilling the mind

a cup of tea waits at the table,
steeped leaves of mint and holy basil

such pleasure in this simple moment
late at night before writing this very poem.

## Time Is a Mystery

Time is a mystery
      standing still as a glassy pond,
      or bending like river water
      curving smoothly over rounded stones

      never and forever
      slow and racing

      always tied to an observer
      like a kite string
      tugging at a paper dot
      fluttering and distant
      in the deep blue sky

With time, everything arises, intermingled
      in an instant of awareness

Time dissolves in late night's dreaming,
      or flashes like lightning
      to display long-lost memories
      some distance from the springs of Lethe

Time is wild, untamed, escaping capture,
      until the viewer's lights
      are once again extinguished

from

*Fragrant Blossoms, Fading Light*

## Contented Little Poet

When the turtle understood
      it could not be a coyote,
      its envy faded

Turtle felt the freedom
      to resume
      being a turtle

Turtle said, "Good for coyote
      to be a coyote"

Turtle could see daisies
      and gophers
      being daisies and gophers

Simple recognition
      from a little poet
      disguised as turtle

Writing little poet poems
      close to the ground
      not in lofty clouds

Seeing simple truths, one at a time
      traveling slowly, carrying home
      place to place, opening gates,
      like little hearts

Turning over little pebbles,
      seeing what lies beneath,
      contented in the little peaceful moments
      as a little turtle poet.

## Witness to the Conservation of Matter

The weight of all the flowers
    and the sorrows of fallen smiles
    fall against the mountain's shadows

Evening spreads across the valleys
    we all share, from ancient beginnings
    to the fresh springs that nourish today's travelers

From morning's seed to faded bloom at nightfall
    the imprints of all we know
    are laid in place and then erased

Even the sweetest meadow blooms
    are composed of the earth's oldest ash
    cycled again in all we touch and see

From our love's soft curving lips to the mottled bark of sycamore,
    all are shaped by this earth's thinnest layer,
    coming into view for this moment's eyes

We live in a narrow band of time, with all its overlapping layers,
    able to see with wonder and awe
    the laws contained in the blooms and their necessary fading.

## We, Too, Wispy Passing Cloud

What a privilege it is
to sit here in comfort
looking to the forested hillside
with clouds passing overhead

The thickness of fragrant junipers
all grown from seed,
windblown or dropped by birds
perched in their own comfort

Over time, through rain and snow,
conditions just right at this elevation,
a forest spread over old volcanic land

We, too, have come out of our own
dust and mud and trees long ago,
and we, as we are constituted,
had nothing to do with the conditions
that preceded us

But we, too, are like those passing clouds,
appearances only, wispy and windblown,
disappearing against the blue background of sky,
returning to the elemental that, too, is borrowed
        for a time

## The Music of Letting Go

On secular Sundays we worked,
unstruck by lightning or enlightenment;
memories of karma fields fading
like long broken filaments
releasing their strangling grip,
snapping at our coat-tails.

Like net-less trapeze artists
we followed some unpredicted course
without Olympian gods or their replacements
to guide or counsel us, but we were not alone.

We traveled in the comfort of a long retinue
that came before us, casting off the spells
and fears that spun out from campfire incantations
and mountain retreats softening the psyche
into cultic beliefs of a peace beyond death.

In time we recognized the downward slalom
that we could see everywhere,
the course that the mightiest mountains follow;
so we take the pleasures with the sorrows
and smile at our vanities and desires,
cultivated on the long slow glide
down the ladder one rung at a time.

This is not to say we live in constant mourning
for the loss of hope or striving, because
we do enjoy the pleasures of learning
and the tastes that cross these sensitive lips,
but we do not hold on as dearly
as we once did, willing now to let them go.

In a pool I asked a floating woman
how she did it without sinking
and she said it's the simplest
and most natural thing in the world,
then she bent her head back into the water
and spread her arms and legs
and soon she was resting there atop the water
like a contented starfish in the morning sun.

And in that clear blue mountain light
I could see that the secret
was to place the ears under water
and not listen to the noises from above,
allowing the gurgling from the depths
to be the music of this letting go

## Morning Ruminations

One lazy warm day, melting
      in their gravel parade, dog people
      tethered to their owners,
      pass in the dusty sun, ballooning blue bags
      swinging from the only free hand they will ever have.

Deer, delicate stepping, through grassy hillside,
      turtles and frogs quiet in the hot creek,
      mosquitoes swarming after yesterday's breezes.

The old man with torn lungs has reached home by now,
      coughing in his red handkerchief waiting to die.

A little girl is telling her father that she has polka dots,
      black starlings on the lawn, magpies squawking,
      tires on gravel, noisy swirling dust drowning the little voice.

Too numerous to name all that is not happening here,
      even the news of emerging despots and tyrants
      tries to penetrate the cool breezes of this hillside retreat.

Dark smoldering clouds hover over the nearby horizon,
      invisible to the blind, devastating as a tsunami,
      a strangler disguised as the Pied Piper on the march,
         whistling into the graveyard.

Do not seek for riches in the sunken treasures,
      this message learned from gold;
      eschew laziness in the guise of contentedness,
      its own sickness of comfort.

Two great craftsmen died on Route 66,
      farmers on acid, witty quiet glances,
      not laughing aloud,

dancing, playful on camera,
coming from music and word-woven skits.

Old memory fragment floats in,
recognized still as memory,
attending marathon Satie piano performance,
metronome on piano, Vexations all day.

Someday the mind wanderings
and memories will merge
into one indecipherable flowing present,
impossible to separate again
into recognition; what did they once mean?
What were their origins?

Ten percent of all the humans who have existed
in the last two million years
are alive today.

Imagine a prison, a hospital, a school yard
where ten percent of the population
over the long history of the institution
was crowded into the small space
capable of providing for only a few.

And the effects were invisible to the inmates,
the patients, the children,
the mass of humanity
until the smoke filled the ventilator shafts
or the masses were pressed hard
against the chain-link fences,
their faces wearing the waffle imprints
and metal filings
of their confinement.

Sitting in the prison cell, no writing paper
      or reliable memory remaining,
      I try to recall words
      that would stay with me
      if I am ever released:

blue sky
breathe in
      breathe out, yes
      alive
feel
feel something, anything

slowly, slowly open eyes
      heavy, laden by sleep,
      see without naming

this body, seek some glimpse
      of awareness

not too fast, without straining
      feel, touch
      boundaries
      barriers

bones and muscle
      turn to see
      and feel again

hear and see beyond
      this body
      without center
      without walls

sounds from afar
      sights out and above

Every reverie ends,
the neighbor's loudness intervenes,
the chorus of inner voices and images,
      wispy floating smoke
      vanishing;
my clawing hands in the air
      cannot retrieve the course
      of dreamy fragments

a dumb silence returns
      I slump, like sleep
      overcome by lassitude,

waiting for the next pulse,
maybe a thread to connect
      to some earlier
           something before

When did this happen? Just now.
Just a moment ago. It was here, so close.
What if that was the thought I was waiting for?
The one that would. Think hard. Would what?
What would that one thought have done?

What would any thoughts, the whole menagerie,
      have done, as if you had any choice?

Am I still imprisoned? Who is asking?
      Am I asleep? Is this an exercise?
      Is there anybody there to tell me?
      Is there any me to hear my own voice
           repeating the same words
      to bring back some recollection
      if I just shake it loose?

# In the Thicket of Words

In the wooded thicket of words
there are snags and occasional clearings,
confusions and understandings

Around each comforting turn
boulders await, impassable language,
invited trappings of spoken sounds
echoes of lost lives, interrupted pathways,
all the burdens of a world of words

Meanings distorted, wavering in midair, forgotten;
the way the mind unburdens itself
before extinguishing its illusions
in its eroding descent, dissolving ideation

Echoes and shadows, approximations
that never close in on the roots
below the layers of underbrush,
teasing gestures that something
lies just beneath the surface of understanding

The entanglements of the frontal lobe
offering invention and foresight
followed by generations of discontent
no return ticket to enchantment
short of letting go of the mental mapping
one word at a time
        into the wilderness
        of unknown sorrows

## Ceremonial Praise Song

In the dark's egg monicle
luta-brinka foresight

light spondencies tool bricked
fortuna melinka kaloyka

we found gray leyoka seeds
piled agoygka sadeeyo

and in our joy
we forgot seforilda makanoydee

an cried no wayto home,
pleased as poydinka dunes forbinaway
in mild cross-bearings

     \*     \*     \*

Author's transliteration:

We may think we are walking effortlessly
as if we have foresight (and agency)

but there are occasions when we are tool-bricked (non-translatable)
and Fortuna's Wheel catches us off-guard (literally, "in our tracks")

we may (incorrectly) believe we have discovered freedom ("found gray
leyoka seeds")
steeped in the Records of the Mountain ("agoygka sadeeyo")

and blindsided, thus, in our joy and fundamental misgivings ("fiorda
baloka")
we lose sight of "seforilda makanoydee" (The Southern Maize Fields)

and in not weeping on our way home (ref. to death or Motherland)
we are pleased (honored) to see the "Eye of Forbidden Sand
Dunes" (poydinka dunes forbinaway)
in the mild (or tempered) "cross-bearings" (suggesting our collective
suffering)

# A Day on the River

Old man with bent back remembers
it was easier to break wild horses
in the shallow river water

Downstream a fisherman
strikes a fish's head
against the hardness of river stone
before the cleaning

Inside an arc of orange plastic buoys
swimming children are laughing,
splashing in the sandy shallows
of the river's quiet curve

White pelicans glide
on the blue water's stillness
like graceful boats
floating in the sky

Somewhere a boat's engine goes silent
and two men paddle slowly
with their desperate little fishing nets,
sieves against the afternoon current,
not expecting to be rescued

The shiny silvery blue surface
mirrors the clear blue sky
shimmering where they touch
in a thin band of light—
river and sky flowing together
downhill toward a golden dusk

## Across This Divided Land

Passing through
     the old dilapidated towns,
     with their boarded up windows,
     collapsing porches, burned out attics,

and shredded plastic bags blowing in the dusty wind,
     snagged in the chain-link fences
     and dry leafless trees,

we saw little sign
     of activity,
     none of the noisy sound of construction

that plagues so many elsewheres across this divided land

In our travels
     we have seen beautiful mountainsides
     carved and terraced
     so new homes can be afforded the best views

of an increasingly crowded and congested valley
     where noisy roadways crisscross
     like a scarred tattoo
     on the back of a living landscape

Everywhere, the growing and the dying,
     interwoven,

     people crowded together,
     bringing with them the speed and noise,

clustering in their agitated race to security,
     accumulating what they can
     for some future they will never have

## An Enduring Ascent

After a long hike to the base,
        the climb up the mountain really began.

At first, no one was present on the gravel trail,
        only the boulders and steep rock face;
        cactus on the ridge line, shrubby trees in the draw.

Then one or two climbers on their descent
        asked if I had enough water;
        offered advice to stay to the left
            on the steep ascent.

A group of three athletic young people
        scaled past me, then another,
        extending his hand and pulling me up
            over a boulder.

"Hey Pops," he called from above,
        "Take a left here; don't go straight up;
            it's too dangerous."

I chuckled as he waved and vanished around a turn high above,
        while I caught my breath and took a sip of water.
        Hey Pops he had said, with such caring and kindness;

            I leaned against a rock and looked out
            over the distant valley, content and safe,
            with pleasure even in the aching breath.

There is camaraderie among strangers hiking toward accomplishment,
        pulling one another along, sharing water,
        encouraging others on the ascent
        an unspoken ethic, shared and passed on.

In the last challenging scramble up the steep ravine
     a gradual curve toward Flatiron
     a half-mile high, level with the distant clouds,
     looking out over desert valley—ancient sea bed.

In the wide flat expanse of the summit, cool gusts unblocked by mountain
     a freshness to mark the end of exhausting ascent.

A sip of water, a few apple slices from the pack,
     hardly a celebration for the hours of climbing,
     before beginning the descent
     strengthened by the knowing that this was done,
a warm and silent satisfaction
that will be carried into the next trail hike
     and mountain ascent
     with new friends to share the way.

## Planetary Citizens

On the long walk home
we see leaves sprouting from
the only tree on the grassy hillside

As we approach we see more clearly
that among the thickly tangled branches
where swing sets used to hang
young green leaves fan out from the tree's outer surface,
leaning toward the sun

They are abundant and flourishing it would seem,
but we see, too, that a dry burl has established itself
at the base of the tree beneath the wide branching

Along the brittle twisting branches,
dry curled leaves look infected
by a canker from within

The old and drying leaves
are no longer nourished
as they fold and fall in mid-season
from old and heavy branches

The abundant green canopy
shines and glimmers
in the afternoon's setting sun,
concealing its worn and spreading desiccation

This was the tree we climbed in as children;
in our common sharing we knew then nothing of alienation
we knew nothing of poisoned homes
or that we risked losing the foundation
of our childhood world

We claimed no single branch
in our youthful play;
for us the whole wide world,
imagined and real, lay within our grasp.

In those branches we brought
our books of poetry, learning to recite aloud
to the blue sky and passing clouds
and best of all to one another
and to all who were with us
in spirit from around the world.

We are citizens of the world,
abiding by the customs of cafes and bistros,
returning again to these hillside branches
that nourished us in youth,
looking outward, from this spinning orb,
beyond the green enfolding leaves,
beyond the living cloak and dying trunk
that has guided us to the edge
of what comes next.

## When the Watchmaker Died

When the watchmaker died
      we wept, not knowing
      whose intent brought us to tears

We thought, at first, the cogwheels of the mind
      would never turn again

Perhaps, through some evil incantation
      the hands of the clocks would cease to turn
      or spin backwards in every town square

With the coils and springs so taut, we were sure
      we were at the gates of the great unwinding

Our numbers had grown,
intolerance and famine sealed off our hearts
      and borders

In a land of parched dreams
reason melted in the unsheltered sun,

What evil genius was behind this, voices chanted
      in the streets, filling the air

Together, we had unlearned so much,
      riding fear to the gates of superstition,
      people branded in the streets
      like cattle, red-hot fire in their eyes

      and amid the widespread carnage
      we were racing to the Moon and Mars.

\*      \*      \*

Just a bad dream
we told ourselves in the morning

Something had bent time
leading us to believe
in some impending cataclysm
even while we denied its presence

We would walk with a more stooped gait,
and we would never trust one another
as we once did, even amid the jovial laughter,
feigning so convincingly that we came to forget
our own nightmares

for a time.

    \*        \*        \*

Amid the lakes
and the distant snow-capped mountains
one could almost forget there was a world
where hearts were breaking
and life itself was recoiling into extinction

Fragrant sweet clover cut in late spring rows,
trucks loaded with green bales of alfalfa
lumbering along the winding highways
in the golden morning light.

Is there anyone in the fields with their easels
to render beauty and peace in paint or song?

    \*        \*        \*

There were undercurrents
        first of peaceful sounds

tones of lingering sadness
      a violin moving through meadows
      a girl, pensive, standing in her long dress
      her high leather boots secure


    *        *        *


The third generation of explorers
on Mars knew no direct contact with Earth;
      there were few elders
      and no conquest of indigenous people
      to recount or dispel

Their history was a mythology cast in red dust
      revolving around the swirl of cold and dark seasons

No watchmaker or Edenic garden would have been conceived
      to describe such a barren world

Outside the cocoon of their suits and capsule
      a lifeless world of potential called
      for a new kind of adaptation

No pollinator bees would alight on blooms,
      no nectar shared, honey tasted,
      or mead-inspired poems crafted

What words would be shared at such distance
      beyond the practical maintenance needs
      and well wishing?

No more appellation of "beloved friend"
      no epistolary exchanges with earthbound survivors
      no sweet smell of blossoms beyond their helmeted screens
      no more talk of apocalypse among the suffocating captives

133

To read our poets anew
knowing that not only the books will vanish
but so too the air and water
the very underlayment
of all that we took for granted

The revivification of longing in a time of loss,
knowing that all the fractures and divisions
are nothing in light of the loss of all
that we have come to cherish

The unfolding course flows with an inevitability,
de-centering hominins and all their artifacts

Faced with such understanding, the searing lesson of impermanence,
on a scale that includes the end of everything
do we cherish or will we disconnect;
do we find compassion or burn in flames of ignorance

*       *       *

There are windows through which we yearn to see worlds beyond,
        even while we neglect the comfort of our own musty air

and if by some chance we enjoy a moment in the minty air
        or see a schoolchild jumping rope,
            hear the call of coyotes in the nearby fields,
                or the conversation of neighbors down the lane,

what capabilities there are, waiting to be reawakened,
            to taste in all our discord the sweetness of twilight's nectar
            to look with wonder on the golden light at nightfall.

## The Necessary Occupation

Moving to the edges
of that busy world
and its weighted
      distractions,

there you may find
graceful forms
often at the periphery
      of vision

there to teach
by mysterious
      example

as do warm breezes
      on summer mornings
      in quiet desert
      or pine-scented mountains

birds, too, in their solitary song
      or wild winged flight
      carry with them
      sources of wonder
      to the quiet observing mind

Even the thin green-leafed branches
      windswept and leaning,
      shimmering in sunlight,
      display their learned resilience

But these are not the only examples you need
      to live out the days
      of your deeply examined life

or the reasons
why you move to the farthest edges
of a congested world so difficult
        for you to inhabit,
        and impossible to abandon

the place where the fibers of your being
remain entwined with the conditioning
        that brought you here

When the roots are severed
        and the way back is overgrown
        and unrecognizable,

        reaching deep into pools of compassion
        in the midst of all the flailing
                and spinning round

        can be a lifetime's necessary occupation

## A Life of Words Unspoken

Who writes the last letter home
        the hard chosen words
to those erased by time,
their addresses long given away
        to someone new

There was something to say
        long ago
when we gathered together
        in the sun
        that seemed to shine forever

We held our words
        as if their special meaning
        would break like crystal
        if we spoke them to one another

When years had passed
        we forgot what we wanted to say
        and we believed we all understood
                what our gestures conveyed

And now all our unspoken intentions
        rest with us alone,
        knowing all who came before us are gone,
        as we compose yet another letter
                we read to ourselves
                alone in the late setting sun

## Sleepwalking into Darkness

To be transported
        outside, beyond ourselves
        into distant ethereal realms

This is what we sought
        for those fleeting moments
        spectral and timeless

with a book, held weightless,
        or a movie in a darkened theater
        where all the day's needs
        were invisibly wiped clean

To be catapulted
        out of a dead land
        breeding tiny monsters
        into the comfort of our concrete jungle

Where thought breeds fear
        and artificial intelligence
        rewires all the known circuits
        of our collective consciousness

To be transformed into something golden
        after all the colors had been wiped hue-less
        and every insight we remembered
        returned in jumbled slogans

Take us from our daily dread
        we who take pity on ourselves
        as we pity our neighbors
        with whom we once concocted stratagems
        in the back alleys of our mind

In the panegyric where so many interruptions
        derailed our best intentions
        and well crafted meanings,
        we begged for one single meaning
                that contained all the others

We sought our daily solace
        in believing one anointed leader
        would arrive with flames in his eyes
        and pull on the strings of our deepest hatreds
        and cast our grievances onto the pyre of resurrected miseries

We desired more than all other wishes
        to return to calm and darkened sleep
        where uninterrupted dreams and entertainments
        would numb us once again into accepting
        the fate we demanded and deserved

We were impatient to unlearn
        the wisdom of our ancestors
        and the common civility of the immigrants
                who brought us here

And so we forged in the smithy of our own blindness
        a new nation of sleepwalkers
        who jailed the intelligent, the creative, the forward looking,
        and placed the keys of the asylum
        in the hands of wild-eyed lunatics
        to show us what darkness really looks like

## The Way of Memories

Fern tendril unwinding
    in early spring forest hillside
    little green nebulae unfurling

    from seed to root to seed

Your rounded shoulders shimmering
    on the seashore,
    shifting feet lifting sand,
    a smile curving over the horizon

Hardly a cloud today in the blueness of blue,
    memories squeezed out
    in unexpected reminders
    of our quiet walks in sunlit places

We pressed the pressure points to ease
    the pain that had nothing to do with us,
    like shadows following every move

Days like this, so many days like this,
    a thousand glimpses for each shared occasion,
    the flash of fern, feet on the beach,
        your soft shoulders so close
        I could cup them in my hands

With time, the light has bent the recollections,
    reshaped them into shards,
    glistening like electric sparks,
    here for awhile, then gone.

## Connoisseurs of the Dusty Road

We sought the mountains and deserts

Millions of us, invisible,
      burrowing into canyons
      nestling in lakeside retreats
      wearing the coastline painted red
          along our sleeves

Each with our own shining wagon wheels,
      pots to cook in, nooks to read reports
          of distant decay,

We met in small pods, secret societies
      in mineral pools and hot tubs
      where we soaked in hidden waters,
      sharing our ebullient scripted tales

No one ran away in the rainy night, linked as we were
      to the places of our nurturing;
      we were Van Gogh's gleaners, the grazers,
      connoisseurs of the dusty road,
      curious in our wandering ways, sharing
      furtive glances under the cover of bubbling waters.

We shared our ignorance and wisdom,
      our mistakes that pushed us forward,
          and then we parted.

We grew accustomed to the welcoming smiles,
      parting footsteps in our unacknowledged melancholy,
      knowing these intersections of lives,
      the slow pummeling of the road
          toward a curved horizon,
          the taste of letting go.

## In the Illusion of Self

Each moment
a roll of the dice
not two or twelve, but
      a million directions,
      a million minute, incremental
      influences for wheels to turn,
      opportunities to orbit, winds to blow,
            before an action is taken,
            a decision made,
            a wishful claim to free will and choice

Old spinning orb, throwing out innumerable sparks
along the rails of change, one spark
      landing on this one narrow spindle,
      this one unpredicted outcome,
      this infinitesimal consequence
      of the infinite influences
      pointing toward each single action

And how momentous this one moment is,
realizing that each little intervention
by this person we have become
      is the tendril unfolding toward
            sun and moon;
      the leaf floating downstream
            curling around swirling eddies;
      the genius following its unquestioned path

We are not players on a celestial chessboard;
our roles are not scripted in a cosmic book,
nor did we deserve to be struck by lightning
      or to be born into comfort, riches, or poverty.

In our responses are contained the ten million shapings
of all the ways we respond to every turn
in our lives

Where we look for volition, there are the ten million influences
shaping the actions, the responses, the way we perceive
the conditions in our lives

How we are shaped is not of our doing;
the conditions that precede us are not of our making.
The people we have become is what determines
the way we respond, the way we take action

O' sister, you were gripped so much harder
than I imagined by the disease of addiction
When you asked how did I kick it, I was wrong
in saying that I just decided to end it, cold turkey.
I did not know then that the millions of conditions
were so different for you than they were for me.
And now I talk to the dead, retelling the stories
of our lives together; understanding now
that you were not to blame for the inflictions
that consumed you, so young,
and so long ago

O' son, in the distance the silence of pain,
and in silence the concealment
of so much that might have been shared;
the outer shell holds the scars
of long-harbored loneliness,
battles fought alone;
the eyes reflect the long gray days,
absences accumulated
in a life with not enough love.
Did we run away too far this time?
Did we not try hard enough

to chase you down those early aisles
and share with you more curiosity and wonder
at the wide world we too ran past?

O' mother, who brought me here,
who taught me to please, to seek approval,
to be loved and respected, and who supported
achievements and bathed in vicarious accomplishment,
        proud mother,
        who sought her own dreams
        in the melodies of friends,
my pathetic offering
picked alone in today's meadow of sorrow
is a basket of thorns
when I intended a bouquet of violets,
a painful failure I try to rewrite
        in the poetry of perpetual seeking.

O' father, who taught me by silent example,
the perfection of craft, walking the long straight line
to the goal in winter's snow, finding the coordinates
so easily, using the carpenter's tools for daily use,
I sat for years at the desk you designed and crafted
to teach me where I needed to be in my inchoate craft
of putting words to ideas, as you transformed ideas into wonders of wood.
I marveled at the ways of woodworking, and worked with you for a time
when you rescued me from my wandering, but I did not find as easily as you
the place where I was heading.
In our last shared work together, the wooden railings of impermanence
        held together for a time, while I charted a different course.

O' my Dearest Living Love, my fellow traveler through years of waiting
for a better way, to find now the pains of your waiting,
we seek comfort still in our travels, unmoored from the familiar,
you whose kindest heart you may not see, as others see you,
giving to others and not taking for yourself, except

in the smallest desires and passing pleasures,
I want to give you so much that I cannot give,
except in the glances of gratitude, the smallest gestures,
the brief embraces, and the lightness of shared moments accumulated.
In my quiet and unspoken regrets, I have taken more than I have given,
even in the shared moments where a touch or kind word
would have counted for something.
To my deepest living love, we move together as we did on that first day,
toward some safety in the comfort of each other,
perhaps not knowing where the next day will take us,
but you are the one I want to be with
to share the sunsets and rivers and distant mountains.

Through these loves and sorrows, unfurled in the course of a long life,
the teachings have been contained in the turnings of chance,
the millions of intersecting moments, the unpredicted cascading events,
and all but a few were unremarkable at the time, pushing their way
before the eyes and ears, the tastes and touchings, like a living picture show,
feeding the illusion of self at the center of experience.

And when I stop to ponder that there is no I,
except in the millions of conventional interactions,
there is a whirlwind of dead ends, burrowings in a dark wood
that find no resolution except this:
consciousness emerges, acquires the ability to reflect
within a sea of illusions, unable to find a position
from which to get outside its own limitations;
then, after a time, like all else that emerges,
it vanishes.

## Five Gates of Entry

Long papery snakeskin sheets
draped atop old rusted wire fence,
shimmering desert heat,
tumbleweed skeletons blowing to silent snow
on distant mountains

My eyes rest quietly on the scene
seeing the story of Snake
climbing barbed wire fence
rehearsing for the climb up
distant snow-capped mountain

Or shot for sport and wrapped about
the top barbed strand as trophy or warning
to other snakes who might seek tall mountains

The story did not end well for Snake
so I must turn away to reinvent
the journey, so Snake does not stare in death
at the lofty mountain peaks
eternally out of reach

I, too, feel the mysterious pull of the mountain peak
and the gates and trials I must pass through
as if Snake had one more chance
in the guise of a little old poet
or desert hermit devoted to his craft
of recording how the journey unfolds

One by one the five gates offer openings
to the trail leading ahead,
learning more the modest craft,
receiving more the opportunities
of dwelling a little longer

on the trail leading from base toward summit
or to the vistas along the way
that offer their own rejuvenating reward

So I unwind Snake's dried skin,
flakes breaking off in my hands,
placing fragments and powdery remains
carefully in the small pouch I will carry
at my side, and if I speak aloud at times
in my travels forward, it is so Snake will hear
that we travel together on this noble path,
and when I am silent, it is so I can listen
to Snake's guiding wisdom

# Selected Somonkas

The Somonka style of poetic expression, like the more familiar haiku, has a structure based on the number of syllables contained in the lines. However, unlike the haiku, the Somonka consists of two stanzas called tankas, written as if by two individuals, one answering the other typically in a romantic exchange. Each tanka contains five lines with a syllable count of 5, 7, 5, 7, 7.

## Somonka 1

From this wild canyon
leaping airborn for your love
it seemed possible
that I could glide all day long
waiting for you to join me

From river bottom
I watched you soaring above
pulling my heart upward
to join again in mid flight
as we do each time I dream

## Somonka 2

Far from home I go
where white lotus blossoms grow
in deep blue water
opening in bright sunlight
a pond of smiling faces

I too see the sun
standing with my arms outstretched
a cup of hot tea
simmers for your safe return
bring your sweet smile home to me.

## Somonka 5

Pleasant to sit here
on the forest path with you.
Even with eyes closed
there is joy when you are near.
Sunlight breaks through misty fog.

When I see these trees
I am renewed once again.
Let's cherish this time
that brings us together here
among ancient wooded pines.

## Somonka 7

Walking this canyon
lost in peaceful thoughts with you,
sun shining through clouds,
fragrant scent of cypress pine,
I can ask for nothing more.

The sky has opened
casting streams of light downward;
around the next bend
our warm water pool awaits
to sooth and refresh our minds.

## Somonka 11

Much like the turtle
we carry our home with us
following the sun
seeking the quiet places
taking only what we need

We are fortunate
to be traveling like this.
When we hear the noise
we bundle up and move on
where peace and sun await us.

**Somonka 12**

Like nomads we roam
sometimes on the flat land route
other times we climb
up Superstition Mountain
looking down from Flatiron

I am resting here
with a book and looking up
you say you see me
down here on safe ground waiting
wishing to be there with you

## Somonka 13

If I was the sky
spreading a blanket of stars
followed by sunlight
all your days would be peaceful
after rising each morning

If I was the earth
holding the warmth of your glow
we could pass the time
dancing in each others arms
inviting all to join us

## Somonka 14

Like innocent child
I picked a bouquet for you
Tiny marigolds
When you deserved a garland
Please accept my best intent

From your heart to mine
Loving intentions arrive
I accept your love
Little yellow sea flowers
And our sand dune memories

## Somonka 17

There are those who say
true love will last forever
but if the sun sets
and every season ends
let us not squander our love

We know that love grows
some like redwoods, some like pines
and what starts must end
so we value what we have
in this one precious moment

## Somonka 19

We reflected long
before adopting travel
as a way of life.
Each day I am rewarded
seeing the country with you.

Waking up each day
I get to see something new.
The greatest comfort
is knowing you are with me
living our dream on the road.

# About the Author

Don Langford was born in Ontario, Canada, grew up in Southern California, and has lived and studied in Oregon and Ohio. He earned his Ph.D. at Ohio State University, writing his dissertation on *The Primacy of Place in Gary Snyder's Ecological Vision*, directed by The Ohio State University's poet laureate, David Citino. His published poems have appeared in several literary journals, and his poem "Vivid Dreams, Antarctica," was nominated for a Pushcart Prize. Langford's poetry collections include *In the Light of the Full Moon:Dispersions, Glimpses, and Reflections*; *Songs from Deep Time*; *Dwelling in the Twilight Realm*; *Water Rock Time*, and *Fragrant Blossoms, Fading Light*. He currently spends his days writing poems, hiking, and traveling with his wife, Marlene.